D1327852

91120000350834

Little
Pebble™

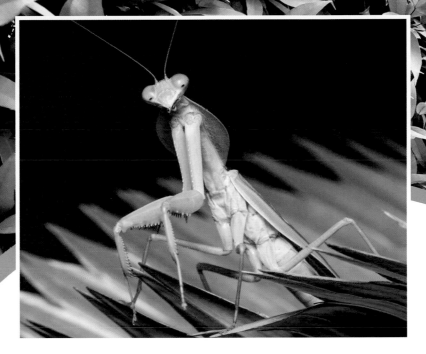

Little Creatures
Praying Mantises

by Lisa J. Amstutz

raintree

a Capstone company — publishers for children

Raintree is an imprint of Capstone Global Library Limited, a company incorporated in England and Wales having its registered office at 264 Banbury Road, Oxford, OX2 7DY – Registered company number: 6695582

www.raintree.co.uk
myorders@raintree.co.uk

Text © Capstone Global Library Limited 2018
The moral rights of the proprietor have been asserted.

Edited by Gena Chester
Designed by Sarah Bennett
Picture research by Wanda Winch
Production by Tori Abraham
Originated by Capstone Global Library Limited
Printed and bound in China

ISBN 978 1 4747 4778 3
21 20 19 18 17
10 9 8 7 6 5 4 3 2 1

British Library Cataloguing in Publication Data
A full catalogue record for this book is available from the British Library.

Acknowledgements
We would like to thank the following for permission to reproduce photographs: Dreamstime: Wxgtupian, 11; Shutterstock: Auschara Roongthanasub, plant leaves background, Eric Isselee, 3, 24, Evgeniy Ayupov, 19, Florian Andronache, 21, iava777, cover, Kristina Postnikova, 13, Lightspring, 5, Muhammad Naaim, 1, Paul Looyen, 9, Rob Byron, 7, Ryan M. Bolton, 17, Valeria73, 15, Yousef Abuaisheh, 22

Every effort has been made to contact copyright holders of material reproduced in this book. Any omissions will be rectified in subsequent printings if notice is given to the publisher.

All the internet addresses (URLs) given in this book were valid at the time of going to press. However, due to the dynamic nature of the internet, some addresses may have changed, or sites may have changed or ceased to exist since publication. While the author and publisher regret any inconvenience this may cause readers, no responsibility for any such changes can be accepted by either the author or the publisher.

Contents

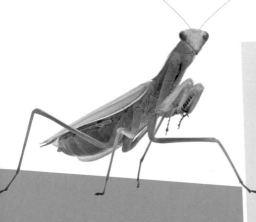

Hiding

Is that a leaf?

No! It is a praying mantis!

The mantis matches a plant.

Hungry animals will not see it.

A mantis turns its head.

Its five eyes see all around.

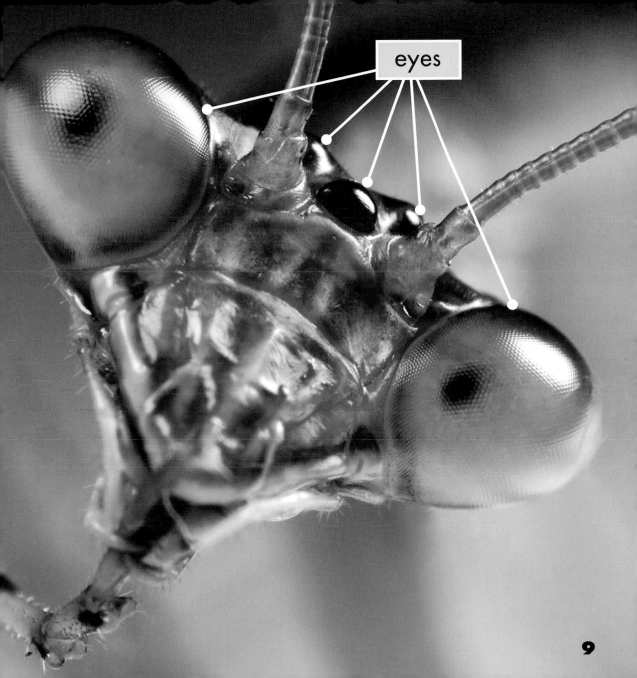

eyes

Look out!

A hungry bat is near.
Hiss! The mantis scares
the bat away.

Good hunters

Snatch!

Spiny front legs grab prey.
They hold on tight. Chomp!

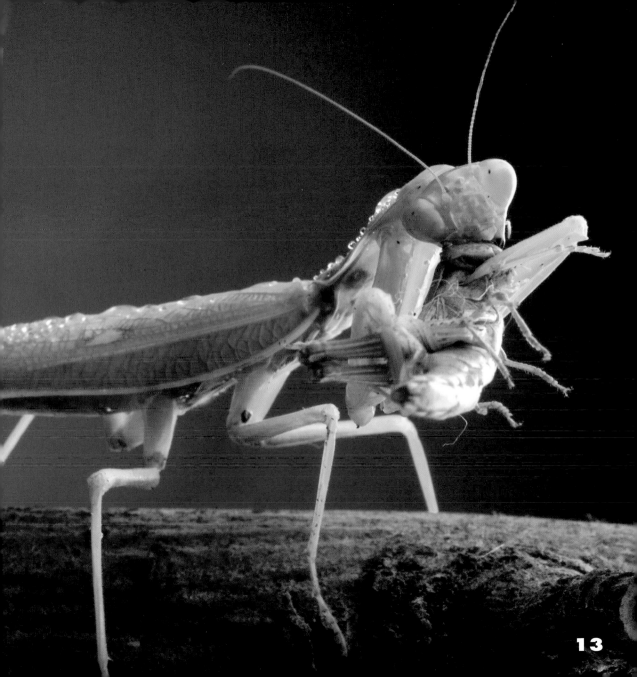

Yum!

Mantises eat bugs.

They eat small birds too.

They even eat each other!

15

Growing up

A female lays eggs on a twig. The eggs are in a case. It keeps them safe.

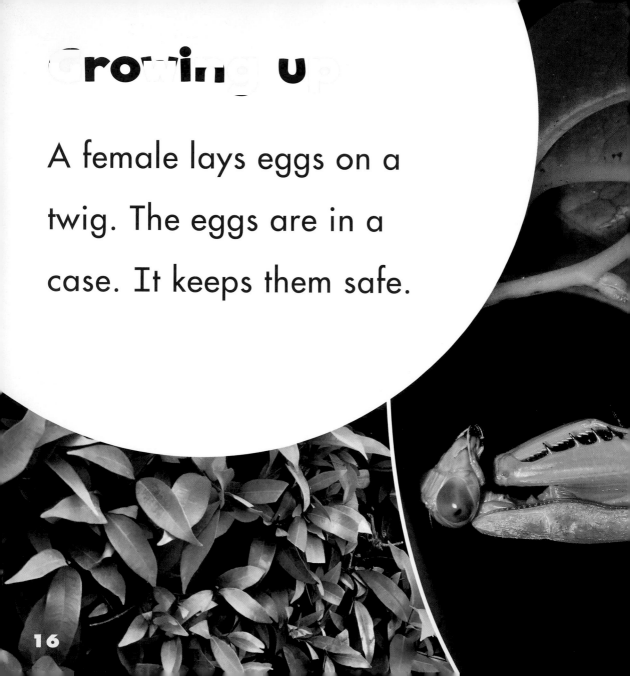

Babies hatch out.

They look like small adults.

But they have no wings.

19

The babies grow fast.
Soon they fly. Bye!

Glossary

adult animal that is fully grown

case outer covering

hatch break out of an egg

insect small animal with a hard outer shell, six legs, three body sections and two antennae; most insects have wings

prey animal hunted by another animal for food

spiny covered with sharp spines

Find out more

Beastly Bugs (It's All About), (Kingfisher, 2016)

First Facts Bugs, (Dorling Kindersley, 2011)

Minibeast Body Parts (Animal Body Parts), Clare Lewis (Raintree, 2013)

Websites

http://www.bugfacts.net/praying-mantis.php
Find out about praying mantises, including where they live, what they eat and what they look like.

www.dkfindout.com/uk/animals-and-nature/insects/mantises/
Learn how many types of praying mantises there are and how they hunt for food.

Critical thinking questions

1. What do praying mantises eat?
2. How do praying mantises avoid being eaten?
3. How is a baby praying mantis the same as an adult? How is it different?

Index